50 Premium Delicious Pizza Recipes

By: Kelly Johnson

Table of Contents

- Truffle Mushroom and Fontina Pizza
- Lobster and Ricotta Pizza
- Roasted Garlic and Caramelized Onion Pizza
- Prosciutto, Arugula, and Parmesan Pizza
- Smoked Salmon and Cream Cheese Pizza
- Fig, Goat Cheese, and Prosciutto Pizza
- Burrata and Roasted Tomato Pizza
- Duck Confit and Fig Pizza
- Shrimp Scampi and Lemon Pizza
- Sweet Potato, Bacon, and Sage Pizza
- Wild Mushroom and Truffle Oil Pizza
- Lobster and Tarragon Pizza
- BBQ Pulled Pork and Pineapple Pizza
- Margherita with Buffalo Mozzarella
- Grilled Chicken and Avocado Pizza
- Black Truffle and Pecorino Pizza
- Caramelized Onion and Blue Cheese Pizza
- Mediterranean Lamb and Feta Pizza
- Spicy Italian Sausage and Roasted Red Pepper Pizza
- Roasted Beet, Goat Cheese, and Walnut Pizza
- Smoked Chicken and Chipotle Pizza
- Peking Duck and Hoisin Sauce Pizza
- Sautéed Spinach, Ricotta, and Lemon Pizza
- Grilled Veggie and Burrata Pizza
- Eggplant Parmesan Pizza
- Bacon, Egg, and Cheese Breakfast Pizza
- Sweet Fig and Gorgonzola Pizza
- Roasted Brussels Sprouts and Pancetta Pizza
- Roasted Pork and Apple Pizza
- Truffle Oil, Mozzarella, and Parmesan Pizza
- Sausage, Broccoli Rabe, and Ricotta Pizza
- Spicy Shrimp and Chorizo Pizza
- Buffalo Chicken and Blue Cheese Pizza
- Prosciutto, Pear, and Blue Cheese Pizza
- Roasted Red Pepper and Eggplant Pizza

- Truffle Mushroom and Prosciutto Pizza
- Roasted Cauliflower and Tahini Pizza
- Braised Beef and Horseradish Pizza
- Sweet Chili Chicken and Pineapple Pizza
- Lobster, Corn, and Chive Pizza
- Burrata, Tomato, and Pesto Pizza
- Roasted Garlic, Spinach, and Feta Pizza
- White Pizza with Ricotta and Sausage
- Calabrese Salami and Fresh Mozzarella Pizza
- Crispy Prosciutto and Fig Jam Pizza
- Spicy Pepperoni and Jalapeño Pizza
- Duck, Mango, and Hoisin Sauce Pizza
- Smoked Salmon, Dill, and Capers Pizza
- Caramelized Onion and Bacon Jam Pizza
- Vegan BBQ Jackfruit Pizza

Truffle Mushroom and Fontina Pizza

Ingredients:

- 1 pizza dough
- 1/4 cup truffle oil
- 1 cup shredded fontina cheese
- 1 cup mixed mushrooms (shiitake, cremini, oyster), sliced
- 1/4 cup caramelized onions
- Fresh thyme for garnish

Instructions:

1. Preheat your oven to 475°F (245°C).
2. Brush pizza dough with truffle oil.
3. Spread fontina cheese evenly over the dough.
4. Top with mushrooms and caramelized onions.
5. Bake for 10-12 minutes until the crust is golden and cheese is melted.
6. Garnish with fresh thyme and serve.

Lobster and Ricotta Pizza

Ingredients:

- 1 pizza dough
- 1/2 cup ricotta cheese
- 1/2 cup cooked lobster meat, chopped
- 1/4 cup mozzarella cheese
- 1 tablespoon garlic butter
- Lemon zest and chives for garnish

Instructions:

1. Preheat your oven to 475°F (245°C).
2. Spread ricotta cheese over the pizza dough.
3. Add lobster meat and sprinkle with mozzarella cheese.
4. Drizzle garlic butter over the toppings.
5. Bake for 10-12 minutes until the crust is golden.
6. Garnish with lemon zest and chives.

Roasted Garlic and Caramelized Onion Pizza

Ingredients:

- 1 pizza dough
- 1/2 cup roasted garlic paste
- 1 cup shredded mozzarella cheese
- 1/4 cup caramelized onions
- Fresh rosemary for garnish

Instructions:

1. Preheat your oven to 475°F (245°C).
2. Spread roasted garlic paste over the pizza dough.
3. Add mozzarella cheese and caramelized onions.
4. Bake for 10-12 minutes until the crust is golden.
5. Garnish with fresh rosemary and serve.

Prosciutto, Arugula, and Parmesan Pizza

Ingredients:

- 1 pizza dough
- 1/2 cup tomato sauce
- 1 cup shredded mozzarella cheese
- 4 slices of prosciutto
- 1 cup fresh arugula
- 1/4 cup shaved Parmesan cheese

Instructions:

1. Preheat your oven to 475°F (245°C).
2. Spread tomato sauce over the pizza dough and top with mozzarella cheese.
3. Bake for 10-12 minutes until the crust is golden.
4. Top the baked pizza with prosciutto, arugula, and Parmesan.
5. Serve immediately.

Smoked Salmon and Cream Cheese Pizza

Ingredients:

- 1 pizza dough
- 1/4 cup cream cheese
- 1/4 cup red onion, thinly sliced
- 4 oz smoked salmon
- Capers and fresh dill for garnish

Instructions:

1. Preheat your oven to 475°F (245°C).
2. Spread cream cheese over the pizza dough.
3. Add red onion and bake for 10-12 minutes.
4. Once out of the oven, top with smoked salmon, capers, and dill.
5. Serve immediately.

Fig, Goat Cheese, and Prosciutto Pizza

Ingredients:

- 1 pizza dough
- 1/4 cup fig jam
- 1/2 cup goat cheese, crumbled
- 4 slices of prosciutto
- 1/4 cup arugula
- Balsamic glaze for drizzling

Instructions:

1. Preheat your oven to 475°F (245°C).
2. Spread fig jam over the pizza dough.
3. Add goat cheese and bake for 10-12 minutes.
4. Top the baked pizza with prosciutto and arugula.
5. Drizzle with balsamic glaze before serving.

Burrata and Roasted Tomato Pizza

Ingredients:

- 1 pizza dough
- 1/4 cup tomato sauce
- 1 cup roasted cherry tomatoes
- 1 ball of burrata cheese
- Fresh basil leaves for garnish

Instructions:

1. Preheat your oven to 475°F (245°C).
2. Spread tomato sauce over the pizza dough.
3. Top with roasted tomatoes and bake for 10-12 minutes.
4. Tear burrata over the baked pizza and garnish with basil.
5. Serve immediately.

Duck Confit and Fig Pizza

Ingredients:

- 1 pizza dough
- 1/4 cup fig jam
- 1/2 cup shredded duck confit
- 1/2 cup fontina cheese
- 1/4 cup caramelized onions

Instructions:

1. Preheat your oven to 475°F (245°C).
2. Spread fig jam over the pizza dough.
3. Top with duck confit, fontina cheese, and caramelized onions.
4. Bake for 10-12 minutes until the crust is golden and the cheese is melted.
5. Serve warm and enjoy.

Shrimp Scampi and Lemon Pizza

Ingredients:

- 1 pizza dough
- 2 tablespoons olive oil
- 1 cup cooked shrimp
- 2 garlic cloves, minced
- 1/4 teaspoon red pepper flakes
- 1/2 cup shredded mozzarella cheese
- Lemon zest and parsley for garnish

Instructions:

1. Preheat your oven to 475°F (245°C).
2. Brush olive oil over the pizza dough.
3. Toss shrimp with garlic and red pepper flakes, then distribute evenly over the dough.
4. Sprinkle with mozzarella cheese.
5. Bake for 10-12 minutes until the crust is golden.
6. Garnish with lemon zest and parsley.

Sweet Potato, Bacon, and Sage Pizza

Ingredients:

- 1 pizza dough
- 1/2 cup mashed roasted sweet potato
- 4 slices of cooked bacon, crumbled
- 1/4 cup shredded mozzarella cheese
- Fresh sage leaves

Instructions:

1. Preheat your oven to 475°F (245°C).
2. Spread the sweet potato mash over the pizza dough.
3. Add bacon and mozzarella cheese.
4. Bake for 10-12 minutes until the crust is golden.
5. Garnish with fresh sage leaves before serving.

Wild Mushroom and Truffle Oil Pizza

Ingredients:

- 1 pizza dough
- 1 tablespoon truffle oil
- 1 cup wild mushrooms (shiitake, oyster, chanterelle), sliced
- 1/4 cup shredded Gruyère cheese
- Fresh thyme for garnish

Instructions:

1. Preheat your oven to 475°F (245°C).
2. Brush the pizza dough with truffle oil.
3. Arrange mushrooms and sprinkle Gruyère cheese on top.
4. Bake for 10-12 minutes until the crust is golden.
5. Garnish with thyme and serve warm.

Lobster and Tarragon Pizza

Ingredients:

- 1 pizza dough
- 1/4 cup ricotta cheese
- 1/2 cup cooked lobster meat, chopped
- 1/4 cup shredded fontina cheese
- Fresh tarragon for garnish

Instructions:

1. Preheat your oven to 475°F (245°C).
2. Spread ricotta cheese over the pizza dough.
3. Add lobster and sprinkle with fontina cheese.
4. Bake for 10-12 minutes until the crust is golden.
5. Garnish with fresh tarragon and serve.

BBQ Pulled Pork and Pineapple Pizza

Ingredients:

- 1 pizza dough
- 1/4 cup BBQ sauce
- 1/2 cup pulled pork
- 1/4 cup pineapple chunks
- 1/4 cup shredded mozzarella cheese
- Fresh cilantro for garnish

Instructions:

1. Preheat your oven to 475°F (245°C).
2. Spread BBQ sauce over the pizza dough.
3. Add pulled pork, pineapple chunks, and mozzarella cheese.
4. Bake for 10-12 minutes until the crust is golden.
5. Garnish with cilantro before serving.

Margherita with Buffalo Mozzarella

Ingredients:

- 1 pizza dough
- 1/4 cup tomato sauce
- 1 ball of buffalo mozzarella, torn into pieces
- Fresh basil leaves
- Olive oil for drizzling

Instructions:

1. Preheat your oven to 475°F (245°C).
2. Spread tomato sauce over the pizza dough.
3. Add buffalo mozzarella.
4. Bake for 10-12 minutes until the crust is golden.
5. Garnish with fresh basil and drizzle with olive oil.

Grilled Chicken and Avocado Pizza

Ingredients:

- 1 pizza dough
- 1/4 cup pesto sauce
- 1/2 cup grilled chicken, sliced
- 1/2 avocado, sliced
- 1/4 cup shredded mozzarella cheese

Instructions:

1. Preheat your oven to 475°F (245°C).
2. Spread pesto sauce over the pizza dough.
3. Add grilled chicken and sprinkle with mozzarella cheese.
4. Bake for 10-12 minutes.
5. Add avocado slices before serving.

Black Truffle and Pecorino Pizza

Ingredients:

- 1 pizza dough
- 1 tablespoon black truffle paste
- 1/4 cup grated Pecorino Romano cheese
- 1/2 cup shredded mozzarella cheese
- Fresh parsley for garnish

Instructions:

1. Preheat your oven to 475°F (245°C).
2. Spread truffle paste over the pizza dough.
3. Add Pecorino and mozzarella cheeses.
4. Bake for 10-12 minutes until golden.
5. Garnish with parsley and serve.

Caramelized Onion and Blue Cheese Pizza

Ingredients:

- 1 pizza dough
- 1/4 cup caramelized onions
- 1/4 cup crumbled blue cheese
- 1/2 cup shredded mozzarella cheese
- Fresh arugula for garnish

Instructions:

1. Preheat your oven to 475°F (245°C).
2. Spread caramelized onions over the pizza dough.
3. Add blue cheese and mozzarella.
4. Bake for 10-12 minutes until the crust is golden.
5. Garnish with fresh arugula before serving.

Mediterranean Lamb and Feta Pizza

Ingredients:

- 1 pizza dough
- 1/4 cup hummus
- 1/2 cup cooked ground lamb, seasoned with garlic and cumin
- 1/4 cup crumbled feta cheese
- Sliced red onions and kalamata olives
- Fresh mint leaves for garnish

Instructions:

1. Preheat your oven to 475°F (245°C).
2. Spread hummus over the pizza dough.
3. Add lamb, feta, onions, and olives.
4. Bake for 10-12 minutes until the crust is golden.
5. Garnish with mint leaves before serving.

Spicy Italian Sausage and Roasted Red Pepper Pizza

Ingredients:

- 1 pizza dough
- 1/4 cup marinara sauce
- 1/2 cup spicy Italian sausage, cooked and crumbled
- 1/4 cup roasted red peppers, sliced
- 1/2 cup shredded mozzarella cheese

Instructions:

1. Preheat your oven to 475°F (245°C).
2. Spread marinara sauce over the pizza dough.
3. Add sausage, peppers, and mozzarella cheese.
4. Bake for 10-12 minutes until the crust is bubbly and golden.

Roasted Beet, Goat Cheese, and Walnut Pizza

Ingredients:

- 1 pizza dough
- 1/4 cup olive oil
- 1/2 cup roasted beet slices
- 1/4 cup crumbled goat cheese
- 2 tablespoons chopped walnuts
- Arugula for garnish

Instructions:

1. Preheat your oven to 475°F (245°C).
2. Brush olive oil over the pizza dough.
3. Arrange beet slices, goat cheese, and walnuts.
4. Bake for 10-12 minutes.
5. Garnish with arugula before serving.

Smoked Chicken and Chipotle Pizza

Ingredients:

- 1 pizza dough
- 1/4 cup chipotle cream sauce (blend chipotle in adobo with sour cream)
- 1/2 cup smoked chicken, shredded
- 1/4 cup shredded mozzarella cheese
- Fresh cilantro for garnish

Instructions:

1. Preheat your oven to 475°F (245°C).
2. Spread chipotle sauce over the pizza dough.
3. Add chicken and mozzarella cheese.
4. Bake for 10-12 minutes until golden.
5. Garnish with cilantro before serving.

Peking Duck and Hoisin Sauce Pizza

Ingredients:

- 1 pizza dough
- 2 tablespoons hoisin sauce
- 1/2 cup cooked shredded duck
- Sliced scallions and cucumbers
- Sesame seeds for garnish

Instructions:

1. Preheat your oven to 475°F (245°C).
2. Spread hoisin sauce over the pizza dough.
3. Add duck and bake for 10-12 minutes.
4. Top with scallions, cucumbers, and sesame seeds before serving.

Sautéed Spinach, Ricotta, and Lemon Pizza

Ingredients:

- 1 pizza dough
- 1/4 cup ricotta cheese
- 1 cup sautéed spinach (garlic optional)
- Zest of 1 lemon
- 1/4 cup shredded mozzarella cheese

Instructions:

1. Preheat your oven to 475°F (245°C).
2. Spread ricotta cheese over the pizza dough.
3. Add spinach, lemon zest, and mozzarella cheese.
4. Bake for 10-12 minutes until golden.

Grilled Veggie and Burrata Pizza

Ingredients:

- 1 pizza dough
- 1/4 cup olive oil
- 1 cup assorted grilled veggies (zucchini, eggplant, bell peppers)
- 1 ball of burrata cheese
- Fresh basil for garnish

Instructions:

1. Preheat your oven to 475°F (245°C).
2. Brush olive oil over the pizza dough.
3. Add grilled veggies and bake for 10-12 minutes.
4. Place burrata on top and garnish with basil.

Eggplant Parmesan Pizza

Ingredients:

- 1 pizza dough
- 1/4 cup marinara sauce
- 1/2 cup breaded and fried eggplant slices
- 1/4 cup shredded mozzarella cheese
- 2 tablespoons grated Parmesan cheese
- Fresh basil for garnish

Instructions:

1. Preheat your oven to 475°F (245°C).
2. Spread marinara sauce over the pizza dough.
3. Add eggplant slices, mozzarella, and Parmesan.
4. Bake for 10-12 minutes until bubbly and golden.
5. Garnish with basil before serving.

Bacon, Egg, and Cheese Breakfast Pizza

Ingredients:

- 1 pizza dough
- 1/4 cup cream sauce or Alfredo sauce
- 4 slices cooked bacon, crumbled
- 1/2 cup shredded cheddar cheese
- 2 large eggs
- Chopped chives for garnish

Instructions:

1. Preheat oven to 475°F (245°C).
2. Spread cream sauce over the dough.
3. Add bacon and cheese.
4. Crack eggs directly onto the pizza.
5. Bake for 10-12 minutes until eggs are set.
6. Garnish with chives before serving.

Sweet Fig and Gorgonzola Pizza

Ingredients:

- 1 pizza dough
- 2 tablespoons fig jam
- 1/4 cup crumbled Gorgonzola cheese
- 1/4 cup thinly sliced fresh figs
- Drizzle of honey

Instructions:

1. Preheat oven to 475°F (245°C).
2. Spread fig jam over the dough.
3. Add Gorgonzola and fig slices.
4. Bake for 10-12 minutes.
5. Drizzle with honey before serving.

Roasted Brussels Sprouts and Pancetta Pizza

Ingredients:

- 1 pizza dough
- 1/4 cup olive oil
- 1 cup thinly sliced roasted Brussels sprouts
- 1/4 cup diced pancetta, cooked
- 1/2 cup shredded Gruyère cheese

Instructions:

1. Preheat oven to 475°F (245°C).
2. Brush olive oil over the dough.
3. Add Brussels sprouts, pancetta, and Gruyère.
4. Bake for 10-12 minutes until crispy.

Roasted Pork and Apple Pizza

Ingredients:

- 1 pizza dough
- 2 tablespoons apple butter
- 1/2 cup thinly sliced roasted pork
- 1/4 cup thinly sliced apples
- 1/4 cup shredded cheddar cheese

Instructions:

1. Preheat oven to 475°F (245°C).
2. Spread apple butter over the dough.
3. Add pork, apples, and cheddar.
4. Bake for 10-12 minutes.

Truffle Oil, Mozzarella, and Parmesan Pizza

Ingredients:

- 1 pizza dough
- 2 tablespoons olive oil
- 1 cup shredded mozzarella cheese
- 1/4 cup grated Parmesan cheese
- Drizzle of truffle oil

Instructions:

1. Preheat oven to 475°F (245°C).
2. Brush olive oil over the dough.
3. Add mozzarella and Parmesan.
4. Bake for 10-12 minutes.
5. Drizzle with truffle oil before serving.

Sausage, Broccoli Rabe, and Ricotta Pizza

Ingredients:

- 1 pizza dough
- 1/4 cup olive oil
- 1/2 cup cooked sausage, crumbled
- 1 cup sautéed broccoli rabe
- 1/4 cup dollops of ricotta cheese

Instructions:

1. Preheat oven to 475°F (245°C).
2. Brush olive oil over the dough.
3. Add sausage, broccoli rabe, and ricotta.
4. Bake for 10-12 minutes.

Spicy Shrimp and Chorizo Pizza

Ingredients:

- 1 pizza dough
- 1/4 cup spicy tomato sauce
- 1/2 cup cooked shrimp
- 1/4 cup cooked chorizo, crumbled
- 1/2 cup shredded mozzarella cheese

Instructions:

1. Preheat oven to 475°F (245°C).
2. Spread spicy tomato sauce over the dough.
3. Add shrimp, chorizo, and mozzarella.
4. Bake for 10-12 minutes.

Buffalo Chicken and Blue Cheese Pizza

Ingredients:

- 1 pizza dough
- 2 tablespoons buffalo sauce
- 1/2 cup cooked chicken, shredded
- 1/4 cup crumbled blue cheese
- 1/2 cup shredded mozzarella cheese

Instructions:

1. Preheat oven to 475°F (245°C).
2. Spread buffalo sauce over the dough.
3. Add chicken, blue cheese, and mozzarella.
4. Bake for 10-12 minutes.

Prosciutto, Pear, and Blue Cheese Pizza

Ingredients:

- 1 pizza dough
- 2 tablespoons olive oil
- 1/2 cup thinly sliced pears
- 1/4 cup crumbled blue cheese
- 4 slices of prosciutto
- Handful of arugula

Instructions:

1. Preheat oven to 475°F (245°C).
2. Brush olive oil over the dough.
3. Add pears, blue cheese, and prosciutto.
4. Bake for 10-12 minutes.
5. Top with arugula before serving.

Roasted Red Pepper and Eggplant Pizza

Ingredients:

- 1 pizza dough
- 1/4 cup tomato sauce
- 1/2 cup roasted red peppers, sliced
- 1/2 cup roasted eggplant slices
- 1/4 cup shredded mozzarella cheese
- Sprinkle of fresh basil

Instructions:

1. Preheat oven to 475°F (245°C).
2. Spread tomato sauce over the dough.
3. Add red peppers, eggplant, and mozzarella.
4. Bake for 10-12 minutes.
5. Garnish with basil before serving.

Truffle Mushroom and Prosciutto Pizza

Ingredients:

- 1 pizza dough
- 2 tablespoons truffle oil
- 1/2 cup sautéed mushrooms
- 4 slices of prosciutto
- 1/2 cup shredded fontina cheese

Instructions:

1. Preheat oven to 475°F (245°C).
2. Brush dough with truffle oil.
3. Add mushrooms, prosciutto, and fontina.
4. Bake for 10-12 minutes.

Roasted Cauliflower and Tahini Pizza

Ingredients:

- 1 pizza dough
- 2 tablespoons tahini
- 1 cup roasted cauliflower florets
- 1/4 cup crumbled feta cheese
- Sprinkle of za'atar seasoning

Instructions:

1. Preheat oven to 475°F (245°C).
2. Spread tahini over the dough.
3. Add roasted cauliflower and feta.
4. Bake for 10-12 minutes.
5. Sprinkle with za'atar before serving.

Braised Beef and Horseradish Pizza

Ingredients:

- 1 pizza dough
- 1/4 cup horseradish cream
- 1/2 cup shredded braised beef
- 1/4 cup shredded Gruyère cheese
- Sprinkle of fresh thyme

Instructions:

1. Preheat oven to 475°F (245°C).
2. Spread horseradish cream over the dough.
3. Add beef and Gruyère.
4. Bake for 10-12 minutes.
5. Garnish with thyme before serving.

Sweet Chili Chicken and Pineapple Pizza

Ingredients:

- 1 pizza dough
- 2 tablespoons sweet chili sauce
- 1/2 cup cooked chicken, shredded
- 1/4 cup diced pineapple
- 1/4 cup shredded mozzarella cheese

Instructions:

1. Preheat oven to 475°F (245°C).
2. Spread sweet chili sauce over the dough.
3. Add chicken, pineapple, and mozzarella.
4. Bake for 10-12 minutes.

Lobster, Corn, and Chive Pizza

Ingredients:

- 1 pizza dough
- 2 tablespoons garlic butter
- 1/2 cup cooked lobster meat, chopped
- 1/4 cup roasted corn kernels
- Sprinkle of chopped chives

Instructions:

1. Preheat oven to 475°F (245°C).
2. Spread garlic butter over the dough.
3. Add lobster, corn, and chives.
4. Bake for 10-12 minutes.

Burrata, Tomato, and Pesto Pizza

Ingredients:

- 1 pizza dough
- 2 tablespoons pesto
- 1/2 cup cherry tomatoes, halved
- 1 ball of burrata, torn into pieces

Instructions:

1. Preheat oven to 475°F (245°C).
2. Spread pesto over the dough.
3. Add cherry tomatoes and burrata.
4. Bake for 10-12 minutes.

Roasted Garlic, Spinach, and Feta Pizza

Ingredients:

- 1 pizza dough
- 2 tablespoons roasted garlic paste
- 1 cup sautéed spinach
- 1/4 cup crumbled feta cheese

Instructions:

1. Preheat oven to 475°F (245°C).
2. Spread roasted garlic paste over the dough.
3. Add spinach and feta.
4. Bake for 10-12 minutes.

White Pizza with Ricotta and Sausage

Ingredients:

- 1 pizza dough
- 1/2 cup ricotta cheese
- 1/4 cup shredded mozzarella cheese
- 1/4 teaspoon garlic powder
- 1/2 cup cooked crumbled Italian sausage
- Sprinkle of fresh parsley

Instructions:

1. Preheat oven to 475°F (245°C).
2. Spread ricotta evenly over the dough.
3. Sprinkle with garlic powder and mozzarella.
4. Add cooked sausage.
5. Bake for 10-12 minutes.
6. Garnish with parsley before serving.

Calabrese Salami and Fresh Mozzarella Pizza

Ingredients:

- 1 pizza dough
- 1/4 cup tomato sauce
- 6 slices of Calabrese salami
- 1/2 cup fresh mozzarella, torn into pieces
- Fresh basil leaves

Instructions:

1. Preheat oven to 475°F (245°C).
2. Spread tomato sauce over the dough.
3. Add salami and mozzarella.
4. Bake for 10-12 minutes.
5. Top with fresh basil leaves before serving.

Crispy Prosciutto and Fig Jam Pizza

Ingredients:

- 1 pizza dough
- 3 tablespoons fig jam
- 4 slices of prosciutto
- 1/4 cup shredded fontina cheese
- Arugula for garnish

Instructions:

1. Preheat oven to 475°F (245°C).
2. Spread fig jam over the dough.
3. Add prosciutto and fontina.
4. Bake for 10-12 minutes.
5. Garnish with fresh arugula before serving.

Spicy Pepperoni and Jalapeño Pizza

Ingredients:

- 1 pizza dough
- 1/4 cup tomato sauce
- 1/2 cup shredded mozzarella cheese
- 10 slices of pepperoni
- 1/4 cup sliced jalapeños (fresh or pickled)

Instructions:

1. Preheat oven to 475°F (245°C).
2. Spread tomato sauce over the dough.
3. Add mozzarella, pepperoni, and jalapeños.
4. Bake for 10-12 minutes.

Duck, Mango, and Hoisin Sauce Pizza

Ingredients:

- 1 pizza dough
- 3 tablespoons hoisin sauce
- 1/2 cup shredded duck meat (cooked)
- 1/4 cup diced mango
- Sprinkle of chopped scallions

Instructions:

1. Preheat oven to 475°F (245°C).
2. Spread hoisin sauce over the dough.
3. Add duck meat and mango.
4. Bake for 10-12 minutes.
5. Garnish with scallions before serving.

Smoked Salmon, Dill, and Capers Pizza

Ingredients:

- 1 pizza dough
- 3 tablespoons cream cheese, softened
- 1/4 cup smoked salmon, sliced
- 1 tablespoon capers
- Fresh dill for garnish

Instructions:

1. Preheat oven to 475°F (245°C).
2. Spread cream cheese over the dough.
3. Add smoked salmon and capers.
4. Bake for 10-12 minutes.
5. Garnish with fresh dill before serving.

Caramelized Onion and Bacon Jam Pizza

Ingredients:

- 1 pizza dough
- 2 tablespoons bacon jam
- 1/2 cup caramelized onions
- 1/4 cup shredded Gruyère cheese

Instructions:

1. Preheat oven to 475°F (245°C).

2. Spread bacon jam over the dough.
3. Add caramelized onions and Gruyère.
4. Bake for 10-12 minutes.

Vegan BBQ Jackfruit Pizza

Ingredients:

- 1 pizza dough
- 1/4 cup vegan BBQ sauce
- 1/2 cup shredded jackfruit (cooked and seasoned)
- 1/4 cup sliced red onion
- 1/4 cup vegan shredded cheese

Instructions:

1. Preheat oven to 475°F (245°C).
2. Spread BBQ sauce over the dough.
3. Add jackfruit, red onion, and vegan cheese.
4. Bake for 10-12 minutes.